RDA WRITTEN & LAW/ETHICS EXAM STUDY GUIDE

+200 Practice Questions

Amy Torosyan RDA, MBA, PMP

RDA Written Exam

Patient Screening & Education – 15% of the RDA Exam will be on this topic – about 21 questions

Covering

- Health History
- Patient Records
- Patient Management
- Blood Pressure
- Physiology of Head Neck & Oral Cavity
- Classification of Caries
- Mouth Mirror Oral Inspection
- Patient Education

What Is Part of the Patient Record?

- Medical & Dental Health History
- Personal Information Form
- Patient Chart – record of key clinical data (charting)
- Informed Consent – written consent - signed and dated prior to the beginning of the treatment
- Dental Radiographs – legal document
- Diagnostic Models – study models – three-dimensional view of teeth and soft tissue

Health History Form

- List of questions about patient past and present medical and dental health history. The purpose of this form is to prevent medical emergency

- Information on medications, allergies and medical conditions that would affect dental treatment. For example, there are conditions that require antibiotics prior to a dental treatment. Should be review prior to a dental treatment

- Should be updated periodically – health status may change

- All questions must be answered by the patient

- Referrals

- Allergies

- Health conditions

- Medications prescribed

- Patient's recall date

- Progress notes on ongoing treatment – need to be documented in INK

- There are 2 types of charting system

2 types of charting system

1) Computerized

2) Manual

RDAs - do not diagnose a condition

- They only chart and document missing teeth, existing restorations, and obvious conditions - Under General Supervision

- DA is responsible for recording the findings of the dentist on the patient's chart

Schematic Drawing

- To document patients' existing condition and pending treatment. Need color-coded pencil to document

- There is a system for calling off the condition of the mouth
    - Start from #1 – 16
    - Moving Down to tooth #17
    - Finish at #32
    - Upper left of the chart is patient's upper right (Maxillary)

There are other types of charting:

- Periodontal charting – records the pocket depth of the teeth (measured by a periodontal probe in millimeters)

- Orthodontic charting – a different type of numbering system is being used

Vital Signs

- Pulse ---> 60 -100 beats / minute (count for 30 sec and double the reading)

- Child pulse ---> 80-100 beats /minute (count for 30 sec and double the reading)

- Rhythm ---> strong, weak, irregular

- Respiratory rate ---> 14-18, child 20-40

- Activity, emotions and breathing difficulties affect respiratory rate

- Factors that cause pulse fluctuations are:
    - Body size,
    - Age
    - Physical act.,
    - Stress,
    - Disease/illness

- Normal blood pressure – 120/80

- Normal temperature – 98.6F

Blood Pressure

- Women and children – have lower blood pressure than men

- Systolic pressure – the higher number/numerator (ex. 120/80)

- Diastolic pressure – the lower number/denominator (ex. 120/80)

- Hypertension - high blood pressure

- Hyperventilation – breathing very fast

- If blood pressure is high – retake the blood pressure after 15 min

- Position of the arm affects the reading – patient should be sitting in an upright position with back supported, feet flat on the floor and arm supported at heart level. Positioning the arm lower - gives higher reading, positioning the arm higher - gives lower reading

Cavity Classifications

- Class I

  Molar & Premolar – Occlusal Surface

  Molar & Premolar – Buccal Surface and Lingual Surface

- Class II

  Molar & Premolar - Proximal surfaces

- Class III

  Anterior Teeth – Proximal Surfaces

- Class IV

  Anterior Teeth – Mesial and distal of anterior teeth (incisal angle) – 2 or more surfaces

- Class V

  Anterior or Posterior - Gingival Surface

- Class VI

  Anterior or Posterior - wearing away or fracture of the cusps - Class VI restorations are commonly seen in upper anterior teeth in the age group of 51 and above) – Cutting Surface

The Gag Reflex

- Is a contraction of the back of the throat triggered by an object touching certain sensitive areas of the mouth or throat

- The sensitive areas vary by individual

- Most often they include the soft palate, the back of the tongue, the tonsils, the uvula, and the back of the throat

  .

Salivary Glands – produce and deliver saliva to the mouth

- Examples of Salivary Glands are:

  1) Wharton's Duct - open into the floor of the mouth

  2) Parotid Glands - below ear

  3) Stenson's Duct - opens at the chick, near upper second molar

Vocabulary (that would help you better understand the exam questions)

- Sinuses - <u>Spaces</u> within the skull to aid and reduce the weight of the skull and is for speech production. (Ex Maxillary sinus – Is above root tips of upper molars)

- Attached gingiva – Stippled and pink – attached to the alveolar process (upper & lower arches)

- Free gingiva – Not Stippled and not attached to any tooth structure, surrounds the neck of teeth

- The tip of the free gingiva is called gingival margin

- Gingival Sulcus – Space between the free gingiva and tooth. (Normal has 1-3 mm depth)

- Frenum – a narrow fold of dense mucous membrane that attached one structure to another
- Enamel is the hardest structure in the body. Covers the anatomical crown of a tooth. It protects dentin and it is <u>inorganic;</u> will not regenerate itself.

- Dentin – located in the anatomical crown and root(s) of the tooth, protects the pulp.

- Dentin has 2 parts:

  1) Primary Dentin

  2)Secondary Dentin

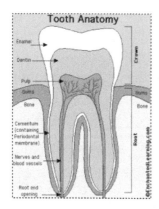

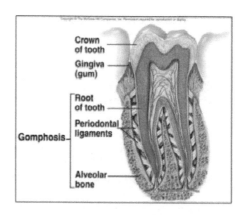

- Pulp – is soft tissue

- Cementum- <u>bone like tissue or</u> calcified substance <u>that covers the root</u> portion of the tooth.

- Cementum – Is <u>connected to the periodontal membrane</u> and is important in tooth movement.

- Periodontal Membrane (ligament) - Cushion between the tooth and the socket (alveolus) in the bone.

- Alveolar Bone – Has Spongy Bone which protects the teeth

- Caries – Tooth Decay

- Abscess- Pus

- Impaction – unerupted tooth

- Malocclusion - abnormal alignment of teeth

- Pulpitis – Inflammation of the pulp

- Periapical Abscess – Small sac around the root tip of an infected tooth.

- Periodontal disease – Inflammation of tissue surrounding a tooth

- Gingivitis – Inflammation of gingival tissues; first stage of periodontal disease

- Vesicle- tissue containing watery liquid

- Ulcer - is a sore tissue

- Macule – Flat discolored area

- Pustule – Small blister or pimple on the skin containing pus.

- Nodules – Raised solid lesion, growth of abnormal tissue

- Fistula – Pathway by which pus forces its way out through the bone

- Hematoma – A mass of blood in the tissue

- Granulation Tissue – New tissue healing

- Leukoplakia- (HIV or Aids patients)- White patch on tissue of the chick that cannot be removed

- Herpes Simplex – Sores on lips, cold sore or fever blister (reschedule pt)

- Torus (Plural-Tori) – Elevation of bone on hard palate or near lower premolar areas.

- Palpation – The use of touch to reveal abnormalities

- Furcation - The place where the roots of teeth fork or separate

- Edentulous – Without natural teeth

Restorative & Esthetic Dentistry 25% - About 35 questions

Covering

- Dental Materials
- Bases, Liners, Bonding Agents, & Cements
- Temporary Sedative Dressing
- Direct and Indirect Provisionals
- Removable Prosthetics
- Bleaching Procedures
- Etching
- Mechanical Matrix For Interproximal Surface Restorations

Bases and Liners (RDA duty) - keep healthy functioning pulp

Bases and liners are used for the following reasons:

- To protect the pulp
- To stimulate the formation of secondary dentin
- Act as a block material between the tooth structure and restorative materials
- To insulate the tooth from electrical or mechanical irritation (Ex. preventing hypersensitivity)
- Bases are:

  1) Never placed on enamel

  2) Never placed into retention areas

  3) Never placed on surface margins

  Note: Always follow the manufacturer's instructions on how to use and store the materials

LINER - Calcium Hydroxide (CAOH)

- Comes in two tubes – base and catalyst

- Compatible with all restorative materials

- Stimulates the formation of secondary dentin (used when cavity is deep)

- Placed on dry dentin – because it is water soluble

- Never placed on enamel walls or retention areas

- No more than 1 mm in thickness

    Note: Allow the material to dry and clean excess with an explore

Cavity Varnish/Liner (Ex. Copalite)
After Calcium Hydroxide & Before Base

- **Note:** Not to be used for composites or resin materials

- Seals dentinal tubules – prevents tooth discoloration from silver filling

- Acts as a blocking agent, blocking chemicals from reaching to the tooth structure

- Varnishes improve the marginal seal between the tooth and restorative material, which prevents microleakage and secondary caries

Application of Varnish

- Uncap the varnish – and never leave the cap off, the material evaporates and leaves a thin film

- Dip small cotton ball into the varnish and saturate

- Apply all the internal walls of the preparation up to the margin

- Gently dry with air

- Need to be applied 2 times

Insulating Base - Protects from Mechanical or Chemical Irritation

- Zinc phosphate is irritating to the pulp and requires varnish prior to this base – Zinc phosphate seals dentinal tubules

- Polycarboxylate cement – non-irritating to the pulp, not as strong as zinc phosphate, could bond to the tooth structure. The consistency should be dough-like

- Glass Ionomer- prevents microleakage, serves as a bond, non-irritating to the pulp, requires the use of an acid etch prior to its application. (Ideal for composite fillings) - The consistency should be dough-like

ZOE (IRM – for deep cavities) – Zinc Oxide-Eugenol

- Placed after calcium hydroxide

- Eugenol – soothes (sedates) the pulp

- Dough-like consistency

- Placing this base – The thickness of this base should not exceed 1 mm

Note: Not to be used for composite restorations

Light Cured Insulating Bases - Urethane Dimethacrylate
RDA – Direct Supervision

- Urethane Dimethacrylate Resin material

- Stronger, faster, and easier to utilize

- Long term release of fluoride to the dentin

- Bonds to the dentin and polymerizes with the composite

- Needed items are:

    - Basic instruments
    - Small ball burnisher
    - Cotton Pledgets
    - Light (20-30 sec as close as possible to the material)

Adhesion of dental materials to enamel is accomplished by:

- Acid etching

- Reaction between two materials – also known as self-curing

Direct and Indirect Restorations
RDAEF duty – Gingival cord retraction & final impressions

- Direct Restorations are: Amalgam Restoration and Composite Restoration

- Indirect Restorations are fabricated outside the mouth: Such as Porcelain Crowns, Inlays & Onlays, Fixed Bridges (pontic – fake tooth, abutment) Porcelain Veneers (requires light cure cementation)

- Removable Prosthetics – Partial and Complete Dentures

- Implants

Etching

- Etching gel - is a water solution of phosphoric acid.

- Etching is applicable on enamel surface

- Etching time - 30 seconds

- Etching increases mechanical adhesion between bonding agents and tooth structure

- Rinse etching gel with air-water syringe for 20 seconds.

Bleaching Procedure

- Soft tissue is isolated

- Hydrogen peroxide whitening gel is used

- Light is exposed for several minutes (depending on manufacturer's direction)

Non-Laser - Home Bleaching Treatment

- Custom-Made Trays

- Hydrogen Peroxide

Mechanical Matrix
DA – places and removes matrices

Types of Matrices

- Tofflemire Matrix System – For Class II restorations

Matrix Retainer Parts

- Celluloid Strip Anterior Matrix – For Class III and IV restorations, forms the proximal surface of the restoration.

- T – Band Matrix – For only primary teeth (baby teeth)

- Head

- Sliding body

- Long Knob (adjusts the band close to the tooth)

- Short knob (holds band in place)

- Note: Retainer is always on the facial surface

Matrix Band

- Small opening of the band is placed on the gingival surface

- Large opening is placed on the occlusal surface of the tooth.

- Matrix band should extend 1- 1.5 mm above the highest point of the occlusal surface. (Too far may obstruct the operator's view or access)

- Band should not extend more than 0.5 -1 mm beyond the gingival margin. (To far will injure the gingival tissue)

- Matrix band placed in the right position – is for the upper right or lower left quadrant feelings
- Matrix band placed in the left position – is for the upper left or lower right quadrant feelings

Wedge

- Pointed side of the wedge - is placed towards the occlusal surface
- Flat side of the wedge – is towards the gingival surface
- Wedges seal the gingival margin of the preparation

Celluloid Strip are used for anterior teeth - DA can place and remove

- Use for Class III and IV composite fillings
- Strip extends 1 mm beyond the gingival margin of cavity preparation
- Strip extends 1 to 1.5 mm beyond the incisal edge of the tooth.
- Ends of the strip should be extended far enough to gasp and pull tightly around the tooth.

Infection Control - 25% - About 35 questions

Covering

- Important Agencies
- Methods of Preventing Transmission of Infectious Diseases
- Dental Unit Waterlines
- Instrument Processing
- Disinfection
- Sterilization

Different Agencies

- **EPA** – Environmental Protection Agency - Protects the Environment

- **FDA** – Food and Drug Administration - Regulates drugs, food, and medical devices

- **CDC** - Center for Disease Control & Prevention - recommends protocols to control transmission of diseases. CDC developed **Universal Precautions** – which requires professionals to treat <u>everyone</u> as if known to be infected with an infectious disease

- California Board of Dental Examiners (**BOARD**) – governs the scope of dental practice – BOARD inspects dental offices for noncompliance

OSHA – Occupational Safety and Health Administration- OSHA is a Federal Agency

- Enforces regulations to protect the safety of employees

OSHA Requires:

- Manufacturers to provide Material Safety Data Sheets (MSDS)
    - MSDS folder should include the following:
        1) A List of materials used in the office
        2) Chemicals found in those materials
        3) The side effects
        4) How to use and store the materials

- OSHA required employers to conduct employee training sessions every 12 months

Methods to Prevent Transmission of Infectious Disease

- PPE – Personal Protective Equipment such as **Gloves**, **Protective Clothing** (changed daily), **Mask** -the *dome-shaped* and *flat types* (change after each patient or when wet or moist), **Shields or Eyewear** – disinfect after each patient.

- Handwashing – 15 – 30 seconds with antimicrobial soap

- Environmental Barriers should be used on surfaces that cannot be easily and thoroughly cleaned and disinfected

- High- velocity evacuation system or rubber dam to prevent prevents aerosol splatter

- Proper use of sharps – one hand method for recapping the needle – EPA regulates how sharps containers must be handled

Protect Lab Technicians from cross contamination by:

1) Rinsing impressions

2) Immersing impressions into a chemical disinfectant. If immersion is not possible, spray with an intermediate level disinfectant

4) Place the impression into a zip-lock bag (mark with hazard label) before delivering to the lab

Hand Hygiene

- Dry hands well - before wearing gloves

- Nails need to be short and well-manicured

- No rings (except for wedding rings), fingernail polish, and artificial nails are not to be worn at work.

- Dental personnel with open sores or weeping dermatitis must avoid direct patient contact and handling contaminated instruments until the condition on the hands is healed.

- For surgical procedures use <u>alcohol-based surgical hand rub</u> after washing with soap

Protective Clothing

- The type of protective clothing needed to wear, is based on the degree of anticipated exposure to infectious materials

- Laundering contaminated protective clothing is the responsibility of the employer

- Protective clothing should be made of fluid-resistant material

- Protective Clothing should have long sleeves and a high neckline. The cuff needs to be tucked inside the band of the glove

- During high-risk procedures, protective clothing must cover at least to the knees when seated

Patient - Protective Eyewear should be used to prevent the following:

- Handpiece spatter

- Chemical spills

- Tooth fragments getting into the eye

Overgloving

- Overgloves - "food handler" gloves, clear plastic gloves.

- Should be worn over contaminated treatment gloves

- Overgloves are used to prevent the contamination of clean objects handled during treatment.

Sterile Surgical Glove

- Worn for invasive procedures; such as oral surgery or periodontal treatment

- Sterile gloves are supplied in prepackaged units to maintain sterility before use

- Health care providers who are allergic to latex can use non-latex gloves

Utility Glove

- Utility gloves are not used for direct patient care

- Utility gloves must be worn to clean treatment rooms and contaminated instruments

- Utility gloves may be washed, disinfected, sterilized and reused

Categories of Instruments

- **Disposable –** one-patient-use only

- **Critical –** instrument that penetrate soft tissue - required heat sterilization

- **Semi-critical –** instruments that contact tissue but do not penetrate soft tissue – required heat sterilize or high-level disinfection for instruments that cannot be sterilized (Glutaraldehyde requires 10hours of exposure)

- **Non-critical –** instruments that contact intact skin – Required intermediate level disinfection with phenol, iodophor or chlorine. Low-level disinfection such as Ammonium Compounds can also be used

Steps Prior To Sterilizing Instruments:

- Scrubbing is NOT recommended

- Soak instruments in holding solution, such as in detergent water or enzymatic solution - to remove blood, saliva, and debris from instruments

- Place instruments in ultrasonic or instrument washer

- Remove and rinse well with tap water

- Examine instruments for broken tips and cleanliness
- Leave the instruments to dry
- Establish corrosion control procedures
- Package for sterilization

Disinfection

- Spray fresh solution over area, wipe with a paper towel
- Spray the solution again and spread it over the area to be disinfected
- Leave for 10 minutes to kill TB microorganism

Care of The Ultrasonic Cleaner
- All PPE should be worn while changing solutions in the ultrasonic cleaner
- The ultrasonic solution must be discarded at least **once a day** or sooner if it becomes visibly cloudy.
- The inside of the pan and lid should be rinsed with water, disinfected, rinsed again, and dried.

Methods of Sterilization

Sterilization is a process in which all forms of lives are destroyed.

The three most common forms of heat sterilization in the dental office are:
- Steam sterilization (the used of distilled water)
- Chemical vapor sterilization
- Dry heat sterilization
- Glass Bead Sterilization for Endo files – Should NOT be used as interim sterilization

Temperature and Time for Heat Sterilization

- Chemical vapor sterilization - 270° F (131° C) - 20 to 40 minutes

- Steam Autoclave - 250-degree Fahrenheit - 20 minutes

- Dry Heat - 320 Degree F - 60 -120 Minutes

Sterilization Monitoring is critical because microorganisms cannot be seen with the naked eye

3 Forms of Sterilization Monitoring:

1. Physical
2. Chemical
3. Biological

- All three processes must be used consistently to ensure sterility
- Biological monitoring - is the <u>only</u> way to determine if sterilization has occurred and all bacteria and spores have been killed
- The Centers for Disease Control and Prevention (CDC) recommends - WEEKLY biologic monitoring of sterilization equipment

Biological Monitoring

- Spore tests ---Biologic Indicators (BIs) are used – BI strips contain harmless bacterial spores (spores are highly resistant to heat)

- 3 BI strips are used in testing: 2 BIs are placed inside the machine. The third BI is set aside as a controller

- The sterilizer is operated under normal conditions with the instruments

- After the load has been sterilized, all BIs are collected and sent for testing

  - Positive result --- a sterilization failed
  - Negative result --- sterilization was successful

Several factors can cause the sterilization process to fail:

- Improper instrument cleaning

- Overload

- Sterilizer malfunction

Special Handling of Dental Equipment

- All dental waterlines and handpieces should be flushed in the mornings and between patients for 20 – 30 seconds

- Although this will *not remove biofilms* from the lines, however, it temporarily reduces the microbial count in the water

- Flushing --- brings a fresh supply of chlorinated water from the main waterlines into the dental unit

- For surgical irrigation – the use of **sterile solution is** recommended

Occupational Safety & Health – About 10% of the exam will be on this topic

Covering

- Modes of Disease Transmission

- Classifications of Hazardous Chemicals

- Waste Management – Types of Wastes

- How to Handle Sharps

- Elements of MSDS – Material Safety Data Sheet

- Knowledge of pre- and post-exposure protocols

Modes of Disease Transmission

1) Direct Transmission – Direct contact with the infected person

2) Indirect Transmission – Contact with contaminated objects or airborne microorganisms. Example: contact with the infected instruments

3) Airborne Transmission - Spread of disease through droplets of moisture containing bacteria or viruses

Transmission of Disease

- Hep B, Hep C – Attacks the liver, The virus is found in blood or certain body fluids – the virus is difficult to kill, there is a vaccine for Hep B – it is given in 3 series; (the administration of the 2nd dose of the vaccine is after a month. The 3rd dose is after 6 months.) Employees are given a free vaccine within 10 days of employment. Refusal form is needed if employees refuse to receive the vaccine

- HIV – Attacks the immune cells, called T-4 Lymphocytes, transmitted through blood, blood products, or other body fluids - HIV virus is not found in saliva – there is no vaccine for HIV – Oftentimes HIV, Hep B and TB are present together

- Tuberculosis (TB) – Caused by a bacteria called Mycobacterium Tuberculosis - Transmitted through the inhalation of contaminated droplets or handling infected tissue. TB is highly resistant to most disinfectants (minimum of 10 hours of exposure is required to kill the TB bacteria)

  - Tuberculosis (TB) active patients are treated with 4 or more antibiotics – non-emergency dental treatments need to be postponed until the patient is not infectious

OSHA Risk Classifications for Occupational Exposure

- Category I – Routinely exposed to known or suspected sources of transmitted diseases – Dentists, DAs, RDAs are classified as Category I

- Category II – Occasionally Exposed – Receptionists

- Category III – Never Exposed – Accountants

- In 1991, OSHA issued the Bloodborne Pathogens Standard (BBP) - It is designed to protect employees against occupational exposure to bloodborne pathogens, such as Hepatitis B, Hepatitis C, and Human Immunodeficiency Virus (HIV)

OSHA requires all employers to provide information on hazardous chemicals to which their employees are exposed to

OSHA Hazardous Communications are:

1) A Written Hazard Communication Program

2) Labels & Symbols Showing the Warning

Radiation symbol

3) A copy of the Material Safety Data Sheet (MSDS) for each chemical (obtained from the manufacturer)

4) Employee Training Session – conducted at least annually

Manufacturers are responsible to provide the Material Safety Data Sheet (MSDS)

MSDS Components are:

- Name, Address of manufacturer
- List of Hazardous chemicals found in the product
- Reactivity data – chemicals that it may react with
- Hazard data- how it affects the body symptoms and first aid treatment
- How to use and store the product
- Recommendations on adequate ventilation and hygiene practices

Interpreting Chemical Labels
NFPA: National Fire Protection Association

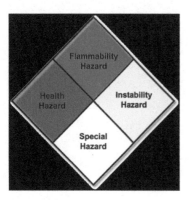

Hazard Ratings

- (Blue) – toxic effect if inhaled, ingested, or absorbed.

- (Red) – the tendency to burn

- (Yellow) – the potential to explode or react violently with air, water, or other substances

- (White) – danger to the exposed skin, eyes and mucous membranes

    Rating Scale: 0 - 4

    0 – Least Hazard

    1 – Slight Hazard

    2 – Moderate Hazard

    3 – High Hazard

    4 – Extreme Hazard

Waste Management

- Medical Waste – POTENTIALLY infectious or harmful material generated by healthcare facilities, such as dental office

- Medical Waste – Falls under the Biohazardous Waste or Sharps as Waste categories

- Biohazardous Waste - Liquid or semi-liquid blood, infectious and/or contaminated materials

- Sharps as Waste – Any device having acute rigid corners, edges or capable of cutting or piercing tissue.

- Handling of Waste – Requires placing it in a container that is sealed

- Waste Containers must be red or labeled "BIOHAZARD" or marked with Biohazard Symbol (in orange or orange red)

Hazardous Chemicals

- Mercury – May cause headache, nausea, fatigue, allergic reaction, irritation of the kidney – toxicity can be acute or chronic

- Acid Etch Solutions – May cause injury to the eye or skin- in case of emergency use eyewash station immediately

- Gasses – Oxygen and Nitrous Oxide are stored in pressurized tanks – Flammable if exposed to sparks or flames

- Alginate Products – Wear PPE when using – Work in well-ventilated area

  Note: Always add powder to the water

Pre and Post Exposure Protocols

- Preventing exposure to chemicals

- Avoid skin contact (even when wearing gloves)

- Wear PPE

- Know how to properly store and handle the chemicals (store gasses away from flame or sparks)

- Ensure adequate ventilation when working with certain chemicals (Amalgam material, Alginates, Nitrous Oxide)

- Ensure proper clean up method is applied – Ex. Mercury spills – require commercial mercury clean-up kit. Do not use the oral evacuator or vacuum cleaner to pick up mercury. **Note**: Clean up Acid Etch spill with baking soda solution

Preventative Procedures – About 7% of the exam will be on this topic

Covering

- Stains, Plaque & Calculus
- Patient Education on Oral Hygiene
- Disclosing Agents
- Coronal Polishing
- Polishing Techniques
- Pit and Fissure Sealants Procedure Steps

Stains

- Extrinsic stains – outside of the tooth enamel – removable by polishing
- Intrinsic stains – inside of the tooth enamel – not removable
- Examples of extrinsic stains are:

  1) Tobacco stains

  2) Yellow stains – due to poor oral hygiene

  3) Green - at the cervical line

  4) Black line stains - most frequently on lingual surfaces above gingival crest

Characteristics of Plaque

- Plaque is made up of bacteria
- Sticky

- Soft

- Forms between 12-24 hours

- If remained on teeth - will mineralize and form calculus

- Soft toothbrush is the best tool to remove plaque - placed at a 45-degree angle against the tooth and towards the gum-line

- Plaque is not easily noticeable - Patients will have a better understanding of plaque if they can see it

Patient Education on Oral Hygiene

- For educational purposes, disclosing agents are recommended to show the effectiveness of patient oral hygiene home care

- Disclosing agents come in the form of tablets, swabs, or a liquid

- Patients chew the disclosing table and swish the solution in the mouth for 30 seconds

- Disclosing agents stain the plaque for the patients to see where they may be leaving plaque routinely

- Disclosing products contain iodine, therefore not recommended for diabetic patients

Coronal Polishing – RDA (Direct Supervision)

- Don't use fluoride paste when preparing for acid etching

- Don't press the cup continuously against the tooth – preventing from heating up the tooth

- Don't polish - on exposed dentin or cementum

- Don't polish decalcified areas

- Polish with a light pressure, continuously lifting to minimize the heat

- Polish away from gingiva

Pit & Fissure Sealants

- Used to seal the occlusal grooves - It is almost impossible to keep the grooves free from bacteria

- Sealant is a clear or tinted plastic-like material, which is applied to the groves of the teeth

- Sealants prevent dental caries most often on the occlusal surfaces of molars and premolars

- Never placed if decay is present

Types of Sealants

1. Self–Cured Sealants
2. Light–Cured Sealants

Procedure Steps

1) Polished with non-fluoride polish

2) Etching – follow manufacturer's directions for the amount of time etching gel is needed to be left on the tooth.

3) The tooth is rinsed off and dried

4) The sealant material is placed in the grooves of the teeth

5) Use light cure for light-cured sealants

6) Check the occlusion with an articulating paper

7) Dentist may adjust the occlusal surface with a handpiece

Note: Most effective method for the sealant procedure is, the use of a rubber dam

Medical Emergency Preparedness - 5% - 7 questions

Covering

- Medical Emergencies

- Nitrous Oxide-Oxygen Equipment

- Administration of Nitrous Oxide-Oxygen

- Basic Life Support

- Emergency Care

Medical Emergencies

- Overdose

  1) Give oxygen

  2) Call 911

- Anaphylactic shock occurs when there is an allergic reaction

  1) Place patient in supine position

  2) Give oxygen

  3) Give epinephrine by injection

- Epilepsy- Uncontrollable muscular contractions and relaxation, a disorder characterized by recurrent episodes of seizures

  1) Protect the patient from falling and from self-injury

  2) Removing from the dental chair and onto the floor

  Prevention: Avoid fatigue/anxiety, make early appointments

Respiratory Complications

- How to help a choking victim

  When the patient is **unconscious**

  1) Put patient on the floor

  2) Attempt finger sweep

  3) Apply firm upward thrust

  Note: If the patient is **conscious**, perform Heimlich Maneuver

- Asthma - histamine is released in the body

  1) Give Antihistamine

  2) Call 911

  3) Give Epinephrine injection

- Hyperventilation – is a condition in which patients start to breathe very fast due to a low level of carbon dioxide in your blood

    - Ask patient to breath in a bag

- Emphysema is a lung condition that causes shortness of breath
  - Oxygen therapy is required

Medical Complications

- Diabetic patients

  1) Ask the patient, when was the last time he/she ate

  2) Avoid stress

  3) Monitor patient

- Angina pectoris – heart is unable to receive enough oxygen. Symptoms are dull aching pain in the chest radiating to the lower jaw, left shoulder, and the left arm

  1) Give nitroglycerin tablet (under the tongue)

  2) Give oxygen

  3) Call 911 if not subsiding

- Anemia – patients have low blood cell counts which impact blood clotting and the healing process

- Scarlet Fever – patients are recommended to take **antibiotics**. Premedication is required prior to their dental treatment

- Rheumatic Fever – patients require to take **antibiotics** prior to their dental treatment

- Artificial Joint – patients require to take **antibiotics** prior to their dental treatment

- Ulcer – chronic anxiety, patients use acid reducing medications. It is important to know the medications before a dental work

- Hemorrhage – excess bleeding occurs – treatment is to give hemostatic drugs such as vasoconstrictor

- Myocardial Infarction – heart cells die

- Syncope – fainting – temporary decrease in blood flow or oxygen to the brain

  1) Remove from humid area (may occur from fear of injection)

  2) Reduce stress/anxiety

Nitrous Oxide & Oxygen Equipment

- Nitrous oxide cylinder – blue in color

- Oxygen cylinder – green in color

- Pressure gauge- indicates the pressure in psi

- Flowmeters – measures quantity of gas being delivered

- Emergency air intake valve- provides atmospheric air

- Nasal hood - also called nosepiece mask

Administration of Nitrous Oxide

- Always monitor the blood pressure and pulse during sedation (RDA duty)

- Check equipment before use

- Start with oxygen - 5 liters per minute, for a few minutes

- Start Nitrous-oxide after oxygen with approximately 1 liter increment. (Range 5-8 liters)

- There should never be more than a 50% level of nitrous-oxide administered

- Inform patients that they may experience a tingling feeling in the hands and feet

- Administered 100% oxygen for at least 3-5 minutes after the treatment is done. Instruct the patient to sit for a few minutes before leaving.

Cardiac Arrest

- CPR – if patient lost vital signs, call 911 and perform CPR

- Call 911, open the airway, listen for breathing

- Give 2 breaths, check for a pulse at the neck

- If no pulse, begin chest compression - 30 compressions and 2 breaths

Dental Radiation Safety – About 5% of the exam will be on this topic

Covering

- Patient Protection Measures
- Lead Apron & Thyroid Collar
- Operator Protection Measures
- Techniques To Minimize Scatter Radiation Exposure
- Film Holding Devices

Dental Radiography
Health Hazards of Radiation

Types of Radiation

- Primary
- Secondary

How to minimize the primary exposure

- Primary (patient exposure) – take good quality X-rays and take when absolutely necessary
- Always drape the patient with a lead apron with a thyroid collar.
- Apron <u>should be</u> stored unfolded
- Each morning run a test film through the processing techniques to ensure that the equipment and chemicals are usable.
- Pregnant patients – first trimester is not recommended to have x-rays
- The lead foil in the film protects the surrounding tissue from unnecessary exposure

How to minimize secondary/scatter exposure

- Stand behind an operatory wall that is either lead-lined or 2 inches thick
- If there is no wall – stand at least 6-8 feet from the x-ray head
- Never hold the film for the patient

- Wear a dosimeter badge. (Normal exposure dose – 5 rems/yr. or 1 ¼ / calendar quarter- operators need to wear all the time - the badge is sent monthly to a monitoring service for evaluation

X- ray holders need to be heat sterilized

- X- ray equipment should be covered with a plastic wrap, foil, or bag barrier

Endodontic Procedures - 5% - About 4 questions

Covering

- Pulp Vitality Testing

- Parts of the Vitalometer

- Procedures of Placing Absorbent Points

- Rubber Dam

- Instrument Grasp and Fulcrum

Endo Pulp Vitality Testing
RDAs may perform

Different Methods of Pulp Vitality Test

- Characteristics of Percussion – **dentist** (tapping)

- Characteristics of Thermal Testing – **dentist** (hot and cold test)

- Characteristics of X-Ray Interpretation – **dentist**

- Characteristics of Manual Electrical Pulp Testing – **RDA** utilizes a high frequency, low electrical current, which is applied to the crown of the tooth. (Vitalometer)

Parts of Vitalometer

1. Probe – (should be sterilized) – Probe is the neck
2. Rubber Tip – Placed on the 1/3 of the facial surface of the tested tooth – should be sterilized
3. Case – holds the battery, should be disinfected. Red light should illuminate when it is on
4. Rheostat – Dial that ranges from 0-10

Pulp Vitality Testing

Vitalometer reading

- Normal pulp – responds to 2-6 range

- Hyperemic pulp- characterized by an increase of blood to the pulp – responds to 1-2 range

- Reversible Pulpitis – can be reversed to normal - responds to 1 -2

- Irreversible Pulpitis – non-vital, cannot be reversed to normal – there will be no reading

- Necrosis of the pulp - dead pulp (non-vital) – there will be no reading

Items for the Vitalometer testing:

- Cotton rolls

- Saliva ejector

- Mouth mirror and cotton pliers

- Electrolyte - toothpaste, fluoride, or topical gel

- Start the rheostat at ZERO

- Advance rheostat SLOWLY

Rubber Dam – Placement of the rubber dam is a Dental Assistant Duty – Direct Supervision

- Bow is placed distal of the mouth

- Rubber Dam Forceps - grasps and holds the clamp from the clamp holes

- Jaw is placed below the height of the contour of the tooth at the gum line

- Clamp is placed 1-2 teeth distal to the prepared tooth (For Root Canal treatments (RCT) the clamp will be placed on the tooth being treated)

- Clamp must be secured with a 12 inch - floss (to be easily retrieved if the patient starts to swallow it)

- Tuck the edges of the dam into the gingiva with a blunt instrument

- Use rubber dam lubricant – to prevent material from slipping through the dam

Rubber Dam Instruments

- Rubber Dam Puncher

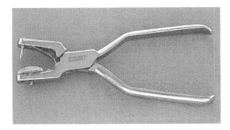

- Rubber Dam Forceps - Used to grasp and place the clamp on the tooth

- Rubber Dam Holder – U shape frame

Endo
Pulpotomy vs Pulpectomy

- Pulpotomy - Removal of a portion of the pulp to help the formation of the root end.

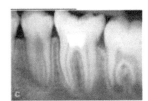

- Pulpectomy - the tissue is removed from the crown and the root of the tooth. Root Canal Treatment (RCT)

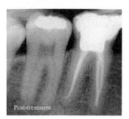

Endo Files, Reamers, and Broaches

- Broach – Removes pulpal tissue

- Reamer – enlarges canals

- Files – To enlarge canals

Drying Endo Canals

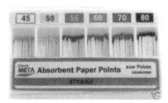

- The Point of the paper absorbent points should be cut 2-3 mm shorter than the working length of the canal.

- Grasp the paper point at the flattened end and place it slowly into the canal

- Leave for 3-5 seconds and remove

- Check for moistness

- Repeat using new points until the paper point comes out dry

Instrument Grasp

1) Palm Grasp

2) Pen Grasp

3) Palm-Thumb Grasp

Instrument Transfer

- Fulcrum (finger rest) – to stabilizes the arm and wrist of the operator

- Transfer Zone – where instrument-exchange takes place

Periodontal & Post Extraction Dressing - 3% - About 4 questions will be on this topic

Covering

- Place Periodontal Dressing

- Place Post Extraction Dressing

Gingivectomy – Removal of soft tissue (inflamed tissue or untreatable pocket) – Requires suturing and dressing

- Gingivoplasty - re-shaping of the tissue due to irregular gingival tissue or enlarged gingival tissue

- Osteoplasty – re-shaping of the alveolar bone- due to irregularities in alveolar bone caused by periodontitis. The process either adds or removes bone to restore normal function

Periodontal Dressing or Bandage

- Periodontal Dressing is needed for the following reasons:

    1) To protect the injured tissue from any trauma during healing
    2) To provide comfort and allow the tissues to regenerate and heal
    3) Prevent from infection or bleeding
    4) Support the mobile teeth during the healing

Placement of periodontal dressing **– RDA duty**

Removal of periodontal dressing **– DA duty**

Steps to remove periodontal dressing:

    1) Dip periodontal dressing in water to lose its stickiness
    2) Make 2 rolls one for the facial and one for the lingual
    3) Irrigate and dry the site with 2" X 2" gauze
    4) Placing – must extend at least one tooth on either side of the surgical site.
    5) Should be smooth
    6) Should be 5-7mm (at least 5 mm)
    7) Place the dressing no further than 2mm from gingival margin
    8) Make sure the dressing is NOT extended further than one-third of the clinical crown

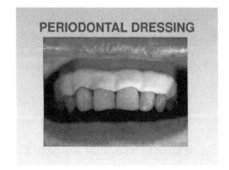

PERIODONTAL DRESSING

Oral Surgery (OS)
Dry Socket – Alveolar Osteitis

What is causing a dry socket?

- When the blood clot did not form after the extraction – leaving the nerve endings exposed

Steps for treating the dry socket – RDA duty under direct supervision

1) Irrigate the socket with saline solution or hydrogen peroxide

2) Dip the iodoform gauze (topical antiseptic to help prevent infection) into dry socket paste

3) Gently pack it into the alveolus with the cotton pliers

4) Inform the patient to return every 1 to 2 days to repeat the procedure

Orthodontic Procedures - 2%

Covering

- Edward Angle's Classification of Malocclusion

- Types of Arch Wires and Separators

- Techniques to Place Arch Wires & Separators

- Orthodontic Bands

- Removable Orthodontic Appliances

Edward Angle's Classification of Malocclusion

- Class I – Normal relationship between the upper and lower teeth and jaws

- Angles Class II Malocclusion – **Dist**oclusion: Mandibular teeth are in **distal** relationship to maxillary teeth

- Angles Class III Malocclusion - **Mesi**oclusion: – Mandibular teeth are in a **mesial** relationship to the maxillary teeth

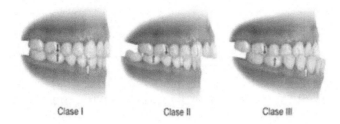

Clase I   Clase II   Clase III

- Overbite – Upper teeth overlap the lower teeth

- Overjet is a type of an overbite – Anterior teeth do not occlude. Abnormal horizontal distance between the anterior teeth

- Underbite – Upper incisors bite behind the lower incisors

- Under Jet is a type of an underbite

- Open Bite – Most teeth occlude but some don't

Orthodontics

.Open Bite – Most teeth occlude but some don't

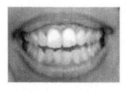

Ortho Separators

There are 3 types of separators

    1) Elastic

    2) Metal

    3) Brass Wire

Metal Separators - are for bicuspid and molar teeth only

Rubber   Metal
Separator   Separator

Elastic Separators - Come in 2 sizes

1) Small for anterior teeth

2) Large for posterior teeth

Placement of Ortho Separators
Placement & Removal – Dental Assistant duty

- Use Separating Pliers to place the rings

- Slide the elastic through the contact area (flossing techniques or knifing action)

  - Lower part of the ring – will be placed below the contact area
  - Upper part of the ring – will be on the chewing surface

Orthodontic Bands

- Thin sheet of stainless-steel bands

Orthodontic Bands

Plain   With Bracket

Types of Ortho Brackets:

- Metal
- Clear

    Note: The slot in the middle of the bracket is for the arch wire

Ortho Archwire – Thin metal that can be easily formed or welded

Ortho Ligatures – Archwires must be secured in place with Ligatures (Elastic rings)

Ortho

. Archwires must be secured in place with LIGATURES

.Elastic rings

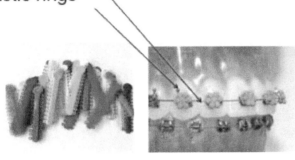

Intra-Oral Arch Measurement Armamentarium -- (Set up)

1) Boley gauge (geydg)
2) Bow Divider
3) Ruler
4) Assorted Pencils
5) Study model
6) Brass Wire

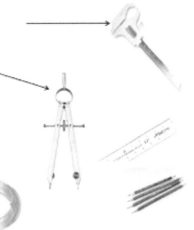

Ortho Springs

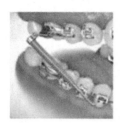 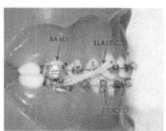

Measuring Arch Perimeter

- Place one end of the wire on the mesial contact point of the first permanent molar

- The other end of the wire should connect to the same area on the opposite side

- Form the wire across the facial surface of the teeth in the arch

- Mark the wire with a pencil at mesial contact points

- Remove the wire and measure the length of the wire between the marks

Removable & Fixed Ortho Appliances

- Springs are used to correct overjet by encouraging forward or backward movement of the teeth

- Hawley Retainers are removable

- Space maintainers are not removable – A fixed lingual canine to canine retainer

Mandibular Incisor Alignment

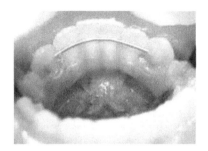

Palatal expansion appliance (not removable)

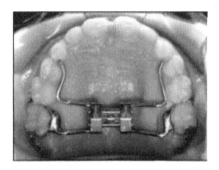

Ortho instruments

- How Plier – Holds the archwire firmly

- Bird Beak Plier – Adjusts and bends the wire

- Three prong pliers – Adjusts and bends the clasps

- Tweed Loop Pliers – Forms loops and springs

RDA Law & Ethics

Patient Autonomy

Self-governance

- Ethical principles state that patients should have the freedom to make choices about their lives
- Dentists should involve patients in their treatment decisions in a meaningful way and treat patients according to their desire
- Upon request of a patient or another dental practitioner, the dentist shall provide any information that will be beneficial for the future treatment of that patient

Nonmaleficence

"Do not harm"

- Professionals have a duty to protect the patient from short or long-term harm
- Keep knowledge and skills current
- Knowing self-limitations and when to refer the patient to see a specialist

Beneficence

"Do Good"

- Personal impairment
- Dentists shall be obligated to become familiar with the signs of abuse and report suspected cases
- Dentists have an ethical obligation to urge chemically impaired colleagues to seek treatment
- It is unethical for a dentist to practice while abusing controlled substances, alcohol, or other chemical agents

Ability to Practice

- A dentist who contracts any disease or becomes impaired in any way that might endanger patients or dental staff shall limit the activities of practice
- May practice areas that do not endanger patients or dental staff
- Must seek physicians help and consultation

Post Exposure, Bloodborne Pathogens (BBP)

- All professionals who become exposed to BBP, regardless of their bloodborne pathogen status have an ethical obligation to inform the health care practitioner for post exposure services. Need to refer the patient for a post exposure service as well

Personal Relationships with Patients

- Dentist should avoid interpersonal relationships with patients that could impair their professional judgment or risk the possibility of exploiting the confidence placed in them by a patient

Neglect or Abandon Patients

- **Negligence** – Legal term used when dentists fail to notify patients that they no longer provide services
- **Patient Abandonment** – when a dentist starts a treatment, he/she should not discontinue the treatment without giving the patient the chance to find an equally qualified replacement

Malpractice

- Improper, illegal, or negligent professional activity or treatment
- When professional fail or momentarily neglect to take responsibility in treating patients properly, causing injury to the patient

Justifiable Criticism

- Patients should be informed of their oral health status without criticizing prior services
- **Defamation** – means the action of damaging someone's reputation
- Dentists issuing a public statement shall have a reasonable basis to believe that the comments made are true

Justice ("fairness") Principle

- Expresses the concept that professionals have a duty to be fair in their dealings with patients, colleagues and society

Principle: Veracity "truthfulness"

- The dentist has a duty to communicate Truthfully
- Dentists shall not represent their services in a false or misleading manner

Representation of Fees

- Dentists shall not represent their fees in a false or misleading manner

Waiver of Co-Payment

- Routine waiver of deductibles and copayments is unlawful, because it results in false claims or overbilling

Overfilling

- The practice of charging more than is legally or ethically acceptable on an invoice or bill

Treatment Dates

- Reporting incorrect treatment dates is unethical
- A dentist submits a claim form to a third party reporting incorrect treatment dates for the purpose of assisting a patient in obtaining benefits under a dental plan

Incorrectly describing dental procedures

- A dentist incorrectly describes a procedure in order to receive a greater payment, or makes a non-covered procedure appear to be a covered procedure

Unnecessary Services

- A dentist who recommends and performs unnecessary dental services or procedures is engaged in unethical conduct

Professional Announcement

- Dentists should represent themselves in a manner that contributes to the esteem of the profession. They should not misrepresent their training and competence

Dental Assistants may NOT Perform the Following Functions

- Diagnosis or treatment plan
- Take impressions for crowns and/or bridges
- Administer injection
- Irrigate and medicate canals
- Adjust and fit crowns and/or prosthodontic appliances
- Surgical procedures, such as cutting soft tissues

RDA Duties – Under General Supervision (Meaning dentist doesn't need to be in the facility)

- Mouth-mirror inspection, charting of existing restoration /missing teeth
- Taking x-rays
- Examine orthodontic appliances
- Placement and removal of temporary sedative dressings
- RDA – inspects and records calculus formation, gingival inflammation, or tooth mobility
- RDA – NOT allowed to check the depth of the gingival sulcus with a periodontal probe

RDA Duties – Direct Supervision (Means dentist needs to be present in the facility)

- Take impressions for diagnostic and opposing modes
- Dry canals with absorbent points
- Test pulp vitality
- Place bases and lines apply topical agents, and fluoride
- Remove dressing arch wires, rubber dams, sutures, matrix bands, ortho separators, excess cement from supragingival surfaces of teeth.
- Bite registration
- Coronal polishing
- Use Ultrasonic Scaler
- Placement of arch wires
- Temporary cementation and removal of temporary crown
- Making temporary crowns

RDAEF Duties – Direct Supervision

- Packing cords
- Taking impressions for cast restorations
- Taking impression for space maintainers for orthodontic appliances and occlusal guards
- Fit trial endodontic filling points
- Clean subgingival surfaces of teeth
- Prepare enamel by etching for bonding

RDA Same Questions with Answers

1	What is the amoxicillin dosage and when should the patient take it?		1000 mg 1hr. after dental work
		x	2000 mg 1hr. before dental work
			1000 mg 1hr. before and 1000 mg 1hr. after dental work
			2000 mg 1hr. after dental work
2	Cavity classification for anterior teeth proximal surfaces is_____.		Class I
			Class II
		x	Class III
			Class IV
3	Labial Frenum attaches the upper lip to the anterior surface of the maxillary gingiva.	x	TRUE
			FALSE
4	After the premature loss of primary tooth, which special fixed appliance is worn to maintain a space for the permanent tooth?		bracket
		x	space maintainers
			headgear
			activator
5	The patient records are: X-Rays, medical/dental health history form diagnostic models, personal information and _____.		invoice
		x	Informed consents
			Patient's chart

				None of the above
6	_____ means that the tooth is in a distal to normal position.			Linguoversion
		x		Distoversion
				Mesioversion
				None of the above
7	_____ means that the tooth is tipped toward the lip or cheek.			Torsoversion
		x		Labioversion
				Transversion
				Linguoversion
8	The system for calling off the condition of the mouth starts from tooth # _____ and goes down tooth # _____ for the lower arch and finishes at tooth #32.	x		#1 , #17
				#16, #17
				#16, #32
				#1, #32
9	Upper left of the chart is patient's _____.			Maxillary Left
		x		Maxillary Right
				Mandibular Right
				Mandibular Left
10	_____ are placed in the contact area, forcing the teeth to spread to accommodate the orthodontic bands	x		Separators
				Ligatures
				Brackets
				Springs

11	Pointed side of the wedge is placed towards the _____.	x	Occlusal surface
			Gingival surface
			Separators
			Gum
12	When the vertical overlap of the maxillary teeth is greater than the incisor one third of the mandibular anterior teeth, this is called?		Overjet
		x	Overbite
			Underbite
			Crossbite
13	An abnormal horizontal distance between the labial surface of the mandibular anterior teeth and the labial surface of the maxillary anterior teeth is called?	x	Overjet
			Open bite
			Cross bite
			None of the above
14	Which of the following is not considered a removable appliance?		Headgear
		x	Palatal expansion appliance
			Retainer
15	What is the normal human body temperature?		68.6
		x	98.6
			89.6
			82.6

16	Factors that cause pulse fluctuations are _____ .		
			Body size
			Age
			Physical activities
			Stress
		x	All the above
17	Hyperventilation is high blood pressure.		TRUE
		x	FALSE
18	Systolic pressure is the higher number and diastolic pressure is the lower number		FALSE
		x	TRUE
19	Which factors can initiate malformation in the unborn child		Genetics
			Environment
			Drugs
			Infections
		x	All the above
20	Fetal alcohol symptoms in an infant are a result of the mother _____ .		Contracting infections
		x	Persisting in alcohol consumptions
			Being exposed to measles
			None of the above
21	What happens when patients' blood pressure reading is high?		Reschedule the appointment
		x	Retake the BP after 15 min
			Give patient blood pressure medication

				Call 911
22	Molar & premolar proximal surfaces cavities are called _____.			Class I
			x	Class II
				Class III
				None of the above
23	Enamel-forming cells are called?			Odontoblasts
				Cementoblasts
			x	Ameloblasts
				None of the above
24	What is the last development stage before eruption?			Initiation
			x	Calcification
				Attrition
				Proliferation
25	What is the final stage of the life cycle of the tooth?			Initiation
				Proliferation
				Calcification
			x	Attrition
26	Class VI Cavities are due to _____.		x	Attrition
				Not flossing every day
				Cavities in between teeth
				All the above
27	The hardest living substance in the body is?			Dentin
			x	Enamel
				Cementum
				None of the above

28	Primary teeth may erupt with a covering over the enamel called Nasmyth's membrane.	x	TRUE
			FALSE
29	Cementum is the bone-like tissue that covers the root portion of the tooth.	x	TRUE
			FALSE
30	Alveolar Bone is composed of _____ that protects the teeth.		Pulp
		x	Spongy bone
			Ligament
			Hard bone
31	Enamel is organic and it can regenerate itself		TRUE
		x	FALSE
32	The pulp is partially made from _____ cells from which connective tissue evolves		Pulpitis
		x	Fibroblasts
			Dentinal
			None of the above
33	The pulp is damaged due to an injury, the tissue may become inflamed, causing.	x	Pulpitis
			Ulcer
			Fibroblasts
			All the above
34	The _____ consists of portions of the tooth structure, supporting hard and soft dental tissues, and the alveolar bone.		Enamel
		x	Periodontium
			Alveolus
			Cementum

35	Mass of blood in the tissue is called?	x	Hematoma
			Ulcer
			Vesicle
			Fistula
` 36	Clinical examination consists of visual inspection of the patient's hard and soft tissue, palpation, checking TMJ, percussion which is _____ process.		Listening
		x	Tapping
			Palpation
			All the above
37	Reversible pulpitis means the pulpal inflammation that may NOT be able to heal itself.		TRUE
		x	FALSE
38	What is the advantages of using a rubber dam?		Provides better access
			Provides better visibility
			Prevents moisture
		x	All the above
39	What kind of safety precaution can be applied when placing a rubber dam clamp on the tooth.		Use 2 X 2
		x	Tie a 12" piece of floss on the clamp
			Use Rubber Dam Lubricant
			None of the above

40	On a dental radiograph, the radiopaque line, or _____ represents the thin, compact alveolar bone lining the socket.		Alveolar crest
			Periodontal ligament
		x	Lamina dura
			Alveolar process
41	What is the difference between gingivectomy vs gingivoplasty?		Gingivectomy is the removal of soft tissue
			Gingivoplasty is the re-shaping of the tissue
			Gingivectomy is done when periodontal pockets are untreatable
		x	All the above
42	_____ mucosa flows into the tissue of the cheeks, lips, and inside the floor of the mandible.		Circular
		x	Alveolar
			Apical
			Frenum
43	Free gingiva is also known as _____.		Gingival sulcus
			Stippled
			Attached
		x	Marginal
44	The mucogingival junction is the line of demarcation between the _____ gingiva and _____ mucosa.		Free, Marginal
		b	Attached, alveolar
			Interdental, alveolar
			None of the above

45	The space between the unattached gingiva and the tooth is the _____.		
			Attached gingiva
		x	Gingival sulcus
			Interdental gingiva
			Marginal gingiva
46	What is the required length when placing a periodontal dressing?		At least 7 mm
		x	Must extend at least one tooth on either side of the surgical site.
			The shorter the better
			It should extend at least 2 teeth on either side of the surgical site.
47	In a healthy mouth, the gingival sulcus space would not exceed _____ millimeters in depth.		3-5
			3-4
			4-5
		x	2-3
48	Which dental specialty deals with the recognition, prevention, and treatment of malalignment and irregularities of the teeth, jaws, and face		Endodontics
			Periodontics
			Oral Surgery
		x	Orthodontics
49	The orthodontic team consists of the_____.		Dentist
			Receptionist and business staff
			Laboratory technician

		x	All the above
50	When placing a periodontal dressing, RDA must do the following _____ .		Irrigate and dry the surgical site with 2 x 2 gauze
			Apply Vaseline on sutures
			Make sure the dressing doesn't extend no more than 2 mm apically or occlusally.
		x	All the above
51	Which of the following is an ideal occlusion relationship?		Class II
			Class III
		x	Maxillary and mandibular teeth are in maximum contact and normally spaced
			None of the above
52	The established system for classifying malocclusion is called _____ classification.		Class I
		x	Angle's
			Pasteur's
			None of the above
53	When performing coronal polishing, RDAs should _____ .		Never press the cup continuously against the tooth
			Avoid polishing decalcified areas
			Use pastes without fluoride when preparing for acid etching.
		x	All the above

54	What is the treatment for Anaphylactic shock?	x	Both A and B are correct
			Apply oxygen
			Administer Epinephrine injection
			Ask when did the patient eat
55	What are the symptoms of Anaphylactic shock?		Skin reaction within 2-5 min
			Respiratory reaction
			Chest pain that radiates to left shoulder and arm
		x	Both A and B are correct
56	What are the symptoms for Syncope?		Fainting
			Anxiety
			Dizziness
		x	All if the above
57	If patient lost vital signs what is the first thing one needs to do before administering CPR?		Find someone who can administer CPR
			Call 911 first if there is no one to call
			Tell someone to call 911
			Both A and B is correct
		x	Both B and C are correct
58	Nonmaleficence is an ethical principle that states _____.		Professional have a duty to protect the patient from short- or long-term harm

			Keep skills current
			Know one's limitations and when to refer to a specialist
			All the above
59	Veracity is truthfulness and it protects from overbilling, waiver of copay, and misrepresentation of care.	x	TRUE
			FALSE
60	When a wall is not available, the operator should be standing at least _____.		2 feet from the x-ray head
		x	At least 6-8 feet from the x- ray head
			At least 10 feet from the x- ray head
			None of the above
61	What are the real hazards of radiation?		Primary radiation
			Secondary radiation
		x	A and B are correct
			Chemical hazards
62	What color is the oxygen storage cylinder?		Yellow
		x	Green
			Red
			Blue
63	Broaches are used to _____.	x	remove the pulpal tissue
			enlarge canals of the tooth
			dry the canals

64	Paper points need to remain in the canal for at least _____.		3 minutes
		x	1 minute
			A and B are correct
			None of the above
65	HIV virus appears to attach itself to a cell in the immune system called T-4 Lymphocyte.	x	TRUE
			FALSE
66	Which custom-made matrix is designed and used on primary teeth?	x	T-band
			Tofflemire
			Spot-welded
			Stainless steel crown
67	If the band of the matrix is positioned left, then it can be used for the _____ quadrant(s).		Upper left quadrant
			Lower right quadrant
			Upper right quadrant
		x	A and B are correct
68	For the young permanent teeth, a pulpotomy maintains pulp vitality and allows enough time for the root end to develop and close. In these cases, the treatment is called?		Direct pulp capping
			Pulpectomy
		x	Apexogenesis
			Avulsed

69	Which procedure involves the complete removal of the dental pulp?	x	Pulpectomy
			Apexogenesis
			Pulpotomy
			Pulp capping
70	Which condition occurs when the teeth are forcibly driven into the alveolus so the only a portion of the crown is visible?		Displaced tooth
			Avulsed tooth
		x	Traumatic intrusion
			None of the above
71	Health care workers should be screened by a skin test for active TB upon employment and at least yearly during employment.	x	TRUE
			FALSE
72	Dentists should report suspicious signs of child abuse to a _____ .	x	Social service agency
			Local police department
			Child protective services
			All of the above
73	Which of the following apply to sealants?	x	Prevent tooth decay
			It's cosmetic
			A and B are correct
			It's a procedure to treat cavities
74	Sealants are placed and the patient is instructed to have them checked once every_____ .		2 years
		x	6 months – a year

			5 years
			None of the above
75	The enamel surface is etched in preparation for sealant. Application time varies from _____.		
			30-60 seconds
			30-90 seconds
			5 minutes
		x	15-30 seconds
76	_____ sealant material is known as self-cure or auto polymerization.		Light-cured
		x	Chemically cured
			Surgical
			Mechanical
77	The height when holding the curing light is _____ mm directly above the occlusal surface.		
		x	2
			6
			4
			8
78	Keeping the sealant procedure area dry is accomplished by?		Asking the patient to keep the tongue still
			Placing cotton rolls on both the buccal and lingual of the working area
			Using Rubber Dam
		x	All the above
79	The application of Pit & Fissure Sealant is performed by_____.		A dentist
			RDAEF
			Dental assistant

			Registered Dental Hygienist (RDHEF)
		x	A, B, and D
80	The tray for the alginate impression material should be enough to include the _____.		The maxillary tuberosity
			Retromolar pad
		x	A and B are correct
			None of the above
81	What accelerates the alginate setting time?		Cold water
		x	Warm water
			Fast mixing
			None of the above
82	An endodontist handles _____.		Oral care in children
			Removal of teeth
		x	Root canal therapy
			Removal of calculus
83	Orthodontics is the specialty of performing		Root canal therapy
		x	Straightening of the teeth
			Extraction of 3rd molars
			Treatment of surrounding tissues
84	Instruments that penetrate soft tissue or bone are considered _____ instruments.		Semi critical
		x	Critical
			Noncritical
			Disposable

85	The specialty concerned with the diagnosis and treatment of the diseases of the supporting and surrounding tissues of the tooth is _____.		Endodontics
			Orthodontics
		x	Periodontics
			Pediatric dentistry
86	Patient sitting position during Alginate impression should be _____.	x	Upright position head tilted slightly forward
			Supine position
			Upright position head slightly back
			All the above
87	Dental assistants should be aware of a patient demonstrating nonverbal communication. Which of the following expressions are considered nonverbal communication?		Facial expressions
			Tightening of hands on the chair arm
			Muffled noise made by the patient
		x	All the above
88	Glutaraldehyde requires up to how many hours of continuous exposure?		2 hours
			30 minutes
			6 hours
		x	10 hours
89	The HIPAA manual must include a job description for each employee.	x	TRUE
			FALSE

90	The office manual must have a HIPAA plan with dates of training for each employee.	x	TRUE
			FALSE
91	To maintain security of personal health information, locks must be placed on all cabinets in the dental office.	x	TRUE
			FALSE
92	The dental office does not have a right to charge for copying and transferring patient information.		TRUE
		x	FALSE
93	OSHA training program is once a year during working hours.	x	TRUE
			FALSE
94	The area of law that clearly defines moral judgment is _____.		
			Civil law
			Criminal law
			Common law
		x	Ethics
95	Intrinsic stains are _____.		
			Removable stains
		x	Not removable stains
			Extrinsic
			None of the above
96	What gives state guidelines for eligibility for licensing and identifies the grounds by which the license can be suspended or repealed?		Dental jurisprudence
		x	Dental practice act
			State board of dentistry
			Statutes

97	Delegated functions that require increased responsibility and skills are called.	x	Extended function
			Dental jurisprudence
			Laws
			Contracts
98	When to perform CPR		When patient has shortness of breath
		x	When patient lost vital signs
			When patient is conscious
			None of the above
99	Black line stains are _____.		Found on lingual surfaces
			It is more often found in females and in children
			Removal may require scaling
		x	All the above
100	Binding agreement between 2 or more people is called _____.		Agreement Letter
			Informed consent
		x	Contract
			Tort
101	Exogenous stains originate from outside tooth and may be extrinsic or intrinsic.	x	TRUE
			FALSE
102	Tobacco stains are ___.		extrinsic
			exogenous

			is yellow to almost black
		x	All the above
103	What is the legal term used for situation in which a dentist fails to notify a patient that she or he can no longer provide services?		Noncompliance
			Abandonment
		x	Negligence
			None of the above
104	The dentist and the dental team members have the responsibility and duty to perform due care in treating all patients. Failure to do this is called _____.		Do good
			Defamation
		x	Malpractice
			Abandonment
105	Tort law protects an individual from causing injury to another person's reputation, name, or character. This injury is called ____.		Fraud
		x	Defamation
			Assault
			Disrespect
106	The area of law covering any wrongful act that is breach is due care, and where injury has resulted from the action is called _____.	x	Torts
			Ethics
			Civil law
			Malpractice
107	In 1992, OSHA established the bloodborne pathogens standard, which mandates that facilities must do which of the following?		Protect workers from infection hazards

			Protect workers from chemical hazards
			Protect workers from physical hazards
		x	All the above
108	General term for the situation in which care is given without intent to do bodily harm and without compensation for this care is called?		Tort
			Invasion of privacy
			Civil Law
		x	Good Samaritan act
109	Under VERACITY principle, the dentist _____.		Need to treat the patient according to the patient's desire.
		x	Has a duty to communicate truthfully
			Cannot abandon the patient
			Should avoid interpersonal relationships
110	Each patient has the right to know and understand any procedure that is performed. The form patients sign that indicates they understand and accept treatment is called ____.		Written contract
			Implied contract
		x	Informed consent
			Implied consent
111	When a dentist sits down and the patient opens his or her mouth, what type of consent does this indicate?		Informed

			Consent form
		x	Implied
			Expressed contract
112	When providing care during an emergency, which of the following should you do first?		Perform an assessment
			Summon more advanced medical personnel
		x	Check for responsiveness
			None of the above
113	CPR should be performed on which of the following victims?		One who is conscious and has an airway obstruction
			One who is having trouble breathing
		x	One who is in cardiac arrest
			One who responds to painful stimuli
114	A fulcrum is a finger rest used by a practitioner to stabilize the hand and reduce muscle stress while performing clinical procedures.	x	TRUE
			FALSE
116	What is the first step of the Cardiac Chain of Survival?	x	Early CPR
			Early more advanced medical care
			Early recognition and access to the emergency medical

			services (EMS) system.
			None of the above
117	You are providing care to a victim having a heart attack. Which of the following would you do first?		Loosen any tight clothing
			Provide comfort to the victim
			monitor the victim's appearance
		X	Summon more advanced medical personnel
118	When performing chest compressions, how deeply should you compress the chest?		About ½ inch
			About 1 inch
		x	At least 2 inches
			Do your best
			None of the above
119	You notice an unconscious adult who was pulled from the water is taking infrequent gasps. Which of the following should you do?	x	Begin CPR
			Check for severe bleeding
			Give 2 initial ventilations
			Continue to monitor the victim's breathing closely
120	Gag reflex areas are the following:		Back of the tongue
			Tonsils
			Back of the throat
			Soft palate

		x	All the above
121	The frontal plane divides the body into left and right halves.		TRUE
		x	FALSE
122	The dorsal cavity is in the anterior portion of the body.		TRUE
		x	FALSE
123	Children who are involved in contact sports should be fitted for _____.		Removable space maintainers
		x	Mouth guards
			Fixed maintainers
			Night guards
124	What does blue color on Chemical Label represent?		Flammability
			Instability
		x	Health
			The danger when exposed to skin
125	Which of the following planes divides the body into left and right halves		Frontal
			Transverse
			Horizontal
		x	Sagittal
126	Which of the following planes divides the body into front and back sections?		Transverse
		x	Frontal
			Horizontal
			Sagittal
129	The sterilization area of the dental office should be near the treatment room.	x	TRUE

			FALSE
130	Dental treatment rooms are also called operatories.	x	TRUE
			FALSE
131	A reclined position with the nose and knees on the same plane may be called a supine position.	x	TRUE
			FALSE
132	Removal of orthodontic bands is performed by _____.		Dentist
		x	RDA
			DA
			Office Manager
133	As a single rescuer you will do cycles of _____ compressions and _____ breaths.		15,2
		x	30,2
			100,2
			30,1
134	When preparing an alginate impression material, you need to add _____ to _____.		Water to powder
		x	Powder to water
			It doesn't matter
			Both a and b are correct
135	The _____ should be well ventilated because of chemical fumes and exhaust from equipment.		Reception area
			Business area
			Treatment room

		x	Sterilizing room
136	An exposure incident report must be taken by the_____.		Office Manager
		x	The dentist
			RDA
			None of the above
137	Normal pulse range for a child is _____.		60-100
		x	80-100
			30-60
			None of the above
138	The special needs patient is defined as a __?		Child patient
			Pregnant patient
			Hearing impaired patient
		x	All the above
139	Smooth transfer of instruments and materials occurs when the assistant can anticipate the operator's need.	x	TRUE
			FALSE
140	The assistant passes and receives instruments with the right hand when working with the right-handed dentist.		TRUE
		x	FALSE
141	Using one hand for instrument transfer frees the other hand for evacuation.	x	TRUE
			FALSE
142	The reverse palm thumb grasp is sometimes called the thumb to nose grasp.	x	TRUE
			FALSE

143	The way an instrument is grasped also dictates how it is exchanged.	x	TRUE
			FALSE
144	The pen grasp is used to hold instruments that have straight shanks.		TRUE
		x	FALSE
145	The modified pen grasp provides more control and strength in some procedures.	x	TRUE
			FALSE
146	Proper instrument transfer is accomplished when _____.		The operators view remains on the oral cavity
			Safety and comfort are maintained for the patient
			Stress and fatigue for the operator and the assistant are reduced
		x	All the above
147	Medical Waste is handled in the following way:	x	Needs to be placed in a container and marked with the Biohazard symbol that is colored orange or orange red
			Needs to be placed in a plastic bag without a label
			None of the above

148	Periodontal dressing can be dipped in water to lose its stickiness before use.	x	TRUE
			FALSE
149	During the placement of an IRM Insulating Base, the desired thickness should not exceed.		2 mm
		x	1mm
			3mm
			5mm
150	The ___ grasp is used to hold instruments that have angled shanks.		Thumb to nose
			Modified pen
		x	Pen
			Palm
152	Acceptable products for hand hygiene is/are		Plain Soap
			Alcohol
			Antimicrobial soap
		x	All the above
153	The minimal handwashing before and after patient care requires ___ seconds.		60
			30
		x	15
			90
154	The ___ regulates the gloves used in the healthcare industry.	x	FDA
			EPA
			OSHA
			CDC

155	What is the name of the agency that regulates disposal of hazardous waste after it leaves the office?		CDC
			OSHA
			FDA
		x	EPA
156	What cycle is perpetuated when pathogens are allowed to pass from dentist to patient or from patient to dentist?		Material Safety Sheet
		x	Cross contamination
			Pathogen standard
			Standard exposure
157	If a dental assistant is hired, who is not immune to Hep B virus, who pays for the Hep B vaccine series?	x	Dentist
			Assistant
			Accountant
			OSHA
158	Updating the patient's health history at each appointment is necessary. Information should be updated both in writing and _____.		Fax transmission
			Over the phone
		x	Verbally
			Email
159	Patients could be infected with HBV and HIV and have no symptoms. This condition called?		Cross contamination
			Antimicrobial
		x	Asymptomatic
			Transient

160	Clinicians should wash hands with either plain soap or an antimicrobial hand wash at the beginning of the workday for 1 full minute. Hands should also be washed when they are visibly soiled, after they have become contaminated, before glove donning, and after glove removal.	x	TRUE
			FALSE
161	An employee who would have any occupational exposure to blood would be a category _____ by job classification	x	1
			2
			3
			4
162	Items in the dental office, such as sterilizers and PPE, are regulated by ____.		
			ADA
		x	FDA
			EPA
			ADAA
163	The healing period for dry socket is usually within _____.		
			2-3 days
		x	2 weeks
			2 months
			None of the above
164	Removal of post extraction dressing is the duty of a Dental Assistant, under direct supervision.	x	TRUE
			FALSE

165	Infiltration injection is mainly used on _____.		Mandibular lower anterior teeth
		x	The maxillary arch
			The mandibular arch
			As-needed basis
166	Topical anesthesia is effective only on surface tissue 2-3 mm.	x	TRUE
			FALSE
167	Materials that are placed directly in the cavity preparation (direct restorative materials) are kept in place by _____.		Chemical retention
		x	Mechanical retention
			Viscosity
			Stress and stain
168	The ability of a material to flow over a surface is called _____.		Viscosity
		x	Wettability
			Luting
			Solubility
169	Dental cements are mixed to a precise ratio. Zinc phosphate cement has reached the _____ stage when the material follows the spatula about 1 inch above the mixing slab.		Etching material
		x	Base
			Liner
			Putty
170	___ is placed as a thin layer on the walls and floor of cavity preparation to protect the pulp from bacteria and irritants.		Base
		x	Liner
			Cement

			Varnish
171	Bases are applied between the tooth and the restoration to protect the pulp.	x	TRUE
			FALSE
172	One of the oldest cements, which comes in a powder/liquid from and is a luting and base cement, is called _____.		Zinc oxide eugenol
			Polycarboxylate
			Glass ionomer
		x	Zinc phosphate
173	When zinc phosphate powder and liquid are mixed, a reaction occurs, and heat is released. The reaction is called _____.		Exothermic
			Mechanical
			Light cure
		X	Chemical
174	When providing care to a conscious infant who is choking, which of the following is most appropriate?		Giving 10 chest thrusts then 10 back blows
			Standing slightly behind the infant with one arm around the chest
			Using the heel of your hand to give the chest thrusts
		x	Positioning the infant so the head is lower than the chest
175	Bonding agents bond to all of the following except?	x	Varnish
			Enamel
			Dentin

			Porcelain
176	Which cement is said to be kind to the pulp and was the first cement that could chemically bond to the tooth structure?		Composite
		x	Polycarboxylate
			Amalgam
			Varnish
177	Adhesion of dental materials to enamel is accomplished by _____.		Chemical reaction
		x	Acid etching
			Mechanical reaction
			All the above
181	Which material dominates the field of aesthetic restorations?		Glass ionomer
		x	Composite
			Bonding agents
			Polycarboxylate
182	_____ gloves are used for patient treatment whenever the dental assistant anticipates contract with saliva or blood.		Poly Nitrile
			Nitrile
			Utility
		x	Vinyl
183	_____ dental cement cures by a chemical reaction between two materials.	x	Self-curing
			Light curing
			Non curing
			Heat-curing

184	Which of the following is a high-level disinfectant?		Alcohol
		x	Glutaraldehyde
			Iodophor
			All the above
185	A _____ is used to condense the base into place on the floor of the cavity.		Explorer
			Spoon excavator
		x	Plastic filing
			Large spoon excavator
186	Cavity liners are placed on the ____ of the cavity preparation.		On the pulp
		x	Deepest portion
			Axial wall
			Gingival wall
187	Which dental dam instrument has a working end that is a sharp projection used to provide holes in the dam?		Clamp
		x	Punch
			Forceps
			Pliers
188	Palpectomy is same as RCT.	x	TRUE
			FALSE
189	Dental dam clamps are designed to be used on a specific tooth. One of the basic parts of the clamp is the arched metal joining the two jaws of the clamp together, called the _____.		Points
			Wings
		x	Bow
			Hole

190	The most used matrix in an amalgam restoration is the _____.			Strip
				Shell
			x	Tofflemire
				All the above
191	Which part of the tofflemire matrix retainer holds the ends of the matrix band in place in the diagonal slot?			Head
			x	Sliding body
				Short knob
				None of the above
192	After the tofflemire matrix is assembled and positioned on the tooth, the band of the matrix should not extend more than ___ mm beyond the gingival margin.			2
			x	1
				1.75
				None of the above
193	Occlusal edge of the tofflemire matrix band should extend no more than ___ mm above the highest cusp.			1
			x	2
				1.5
				All the above
194	BSI is a system requiring wearing personal protective equipment to prevent contact with all body fluids.		x	TRUE
				FALSE

195	Employers must protect their employees from exposure to blood and OPIM during the time when employees are at work.	x	TRUE
			FALSE
196	When a disinfecting solution meets all the claims listed and safety concerns are noted, the FDA will assign an EPA number that must appear on the label of the solution.		TRUE
		x	FALSE
197	Microorganisms may be missed because they appear as a mist or dry clear on the surfaces that are touched.	x	TRUE
			FALSE
198	When removing protective clothing, OSHA states that special care is to be taken with items that are considered potentially infectious.	x	TRUE
			FALSE
199	___ is the principal professional organization for dentistry in the US.		CDC
		x	OSHA
			US public health services
			ADA
200	Name the agency that is part of the US public health services, a division of the US department of health and human services, and a source of many regulations.	x	CDC
			OSHA
			ADA
			OPIM

201	In 1992, OSHA established the bloodborne pathogens standard, which mandates that facilities must do which of the following?		Protect workers from infection hazards
			Protect workers from chemical hazards
			Protect workers from physical hazards
		x	All the above

Endnotes

American Dental Association,
(2022) https://www.ada.org/en/resources/research/science-and-research-institute/oral-health-topics/antibiotic-prophylaxis
Barbara Blade-Jacobs, Kristy S. Borquez. (1997) *"The California RDA Review Manual"* *California*
Center of Disease Control and Prevention, (2021) https://www.cdc.gov/index.htm
Dental Board of California, (2021) https://www.dbc.ca.gov/licensees/rda/renewals.shtml
Food and Drug Administration (FDA), https://www.fda.gov/
Occupational Safety and Health
Administration, (2022) https://www.osha.gov/bloodborne-pathogens
Occupational Safety and Health Administration, (2022) https://www.osha.gov/hazardous-waste
Pixabay, https://pixabay.com/
PSI Testing Excellence, (2021) https://www.psiexams.com/
The ADA Principles of Ethics and Code of Conduct,
(2022) https://www.ada.org/en/about/principles/code-of-ethics
Unsplash, (2020) https://unsplash.com/